EARTH'S CYCLES

The Water Cycle

CHERYL JAKAB

Smart Apple Media

This edition first published in 2008 in the United States of America by Smart Apple Media.
Reprinted 2008

Smart Apple Media
2140 Howard Drive West
North Mankato, Minnesota 56003

First published in 2007 by
MACMILLAN EDUCATION AUSTRALIA PTY LTD
15–19 Claremont Street, South Yarra, Australia 3141

Visit our Web site at www.macmillan.com.au or go directly to www.macmillanlibrary.com.au

Associated companies and representatives throughout the world.

Library of Congress Cataloging-in-Publication Data

Jakab, Cheryl.
   The water cycle / by Cheryl Jakab.
   p. cm. — (Earth's cycles)
   Includes index.
   ISBN 978-1-59920-144-3
   1. Hydrologic cycle—Juvenile literature. I. Title.

GB848.J35 2007
551.48—dc22

2007004550

Edited by Erin Richards
Text and cover design by Christine Deering
Page layout by Christine Deering
Photo research by Jes Senbergs
Illustrations by Ann Likhovetsky, pp. 6, 12, 13, 16, 17, 19; Paul Könye, p. 29.

Printed in U.S.

Acknowledgements
The author and the publisher are grateful to the following for permission to reproduce copyright material:

Front cover photograph: cumulus clouds (center), courtesy of Photodisc; ocean wave (background), courtesy of Photodisc.

Aqua Image/Alamy, p. 10; Robert Harding Picture Library Ltd/Alamy, p. 14; Ausaid Photographic Library, p. 26; Jean-Paul Ferrero/Auscape, pp. 5, 12; Jean-Michel Labat/Auscape, p. 28 (bottom); Corbis, pp. 4 (middle right & top left), 20 (middle left & middle right); Nick Dolding/Getty Images, p. 28 (top); Jeff Foott/Getty Images, p. 11 (bottom); Sylvain Grandadam/Getty Images, p. 21 (bottom); Robert C Nunnington/Getty Images, p. 7; Farhad J Parsa/Getty Images, p. 19; Thomas Schmitt/Getty Images, p. 23 (top); iStockphoto.comphoto, p. 22 (bottom); Jiri Lochman/Lochman Transparencies, p. 15 (bottom); Marie Lochman/Lochman Transparencies, p. 15 (top); NASA, pp. 4 (center), 18 (insert), 30; NASA/Science Photo Library, p. 6; NOAA, pp. 9, 16; Pelusey Photography, p. 27; Photos.com, p. 13; Photodisc, pp. 1, 4 (bottom left, bottom right, middle left & top right), 8, 18 (main), 20 (bottom left, bottom right, center & top), 22 (top), 23 (bottom), 24; FairfaxPhotos/ Peter Rae, p. 25; J&E Richards, p. 11 (top); Lonely Planet Images/Garry Weare, p. 21 (top).

Contents

Rain

Clouds

Rivers and oceans

Water vapor

ideas and tips

Glossary words
When a word is printed in **bold**, you can look up its meaning in the glossary on page 31.

Earth's natural cycles

What is a cycle?

A cycle is a never-ending series of changes that repeats again and again. Arrows in cycle diagrams show the direction in which the cycle is moving.

Earth's natural cycles create all the environments on Earth. Living and non-living things are constantly changing. Each change is part of a natural cycle. Earth's natural cycles are working all the time.

Earth's non-living cycles are:

- the water cycle
- the rock cycle
- the seasons cycle

Earth's living cycles are:

- the food cycle
- the animal life cycle
- the plant life cycle

Seasons cycle

Food cycle

Water cycle

Plant life cycle

Animal life cycle

Rock cycle

Earth's natural cycles keep the planet healthy.

4

The balance of nature

Earth's natural cycles all connect with each other. The way the cycles connect is sometimes called the balance of nature.

Keeping the balance

Every living thing depends on Earth's natural cycles to survive. A change in one cycle can affect the whole balance of nature. Knowing how Earth's cycles work helps us keep the environment healthy.

Every living thing depends on the balance of nature to survive.

Water

What is water?

Pure water is a substance that has no color or taste. Water can be **liquid**, **solid**, or **gas**. The chemical symbol for water is H_2O.

Water in oceans covers nearly three-quarters of Earth's surface. Liquid water falls as rain on Earth's surface and flows in rivers and streams. Water in clouds fills large areas of the sky. Ice and snow are solid water.

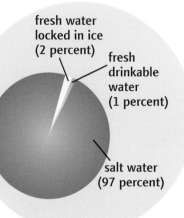

fresh water locked in ice (2 percent)

fresh drinkable water (1 percent)

salt water (97 percent)

Only a small amount of Earth's water is fresh, drinkable water.

Earth appears blue from space, because of the water in the oceans.

The importance of water

Water is a very important part of the natural environment.
Every living thing on Earth depends on water to survive.

Why is water important to people?

People need fresh water to drink. The human body is made of about 70 percent water. People use fresh water to wash, cook, and to grow food crops.

How do people affect water?

People are using up fresh water faster than it can be collected from rainfall. A lot of the water on Earth is being polluted by wastes made by people.

How does water fit into the balance of nature?

Water is essential to every living thing on Earth. Plants and animals need water to survive. Water shapes the coastlines and the surface of the land.

Fresh water is essential to land animals, such as elephants, for survival.

The water cycle

The water cycle shows the different stages of how water moves through the environment. Water falls from the sky as rain, and collects in rivers and oceans. It then **evaporates** from the oceans into the air and **condenses** to form clouds in the sky.

Rain

Rivers and oceans

Water vapor

Clouds

Water moves through the environment in an endless cycle.

Solid, liquid, and gas

Water is one of few substances that exists naturally as solid, liquid, and gas. When water is solid it is called ice or snow. At normal room temperature, water is liquid. When water is gas it is called water vapor. Heating and cooling causes water to change from one form to another.

gas

solid

liquid

Water exists on Earth as solid, liquid, and gas.

Rain

Rain · Clouds · Rivers and oceans · Water vapor

Rain is the stage of the water cycle when water falls to Earth from clouds in the sky. Tiny droplets of water in clouds join up with other droplets to form raindrops. When clouds become too heavy with water, raindrops fall from the sky as rain. Rainfall can be a light drizzle or it can be a heavy downpour. Sometimes it rains for only a few minutes, and sometimes it rains for hours.

Rain falls from clouds in the sky.

Amount of rainfall

Different places on Earth get different amounts of rainfall each year. The amount of rain in a year is called the annual rainfall. A **rain gauge** is used to measure the amount of rain that falls. Deserts have a low annual rainfall, usually less than 10 inches (250 mm). Most **tropical areas** have a high annual rainfall. They get more than 79 inches (2000 mm) of rain each year.

A lot of rain falls in tropical areas during the wet season.

Deserts have a very low annual rainfall.

Rivers and oceans

After falling as rain, the next stage of the water cycle is when water collects in rivers and oceans. Rivers flow downward because of **gravity**. They will keep flowing until they reach the lowest point of the land. Rivers flow quickly over steep areas and slowly in flatter areas. Some rivers flow into lakes and wetlands but most find their way to the oceans.

The mouth of a river is the place where the river meets the ocean.

Rainwater flows down over the land because of gravity.

rain

river

river

flow of water

ocean

Groundwater

Some rainwater seeps through the soil instead of flowing over the land. It collects deep underground between layers of rock, and is called groundwater. In some places, groundwater collects to form massive undergound water supplies.

Groundwater can reappear on the surface in freshwater springs.

Ocean currents

Most liquid water on Earth is in the oceans. Ocean water moves around the world in ocean currents. Ocean currents are like rivers moving through the oceans. Some of the water travels down to the deep in ocean currents and stays there for hundreds of years.

Water moves through the oceans in ocean currents.

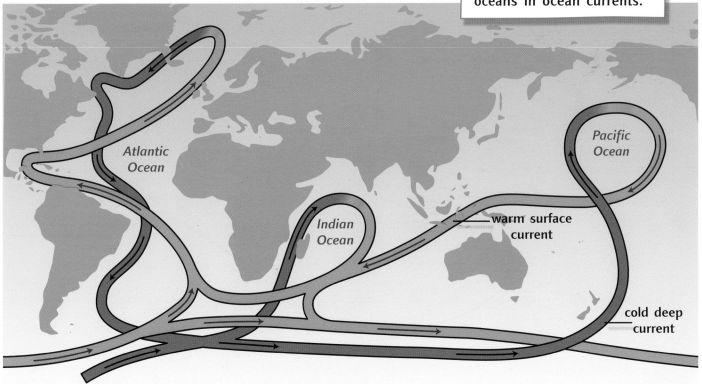

Atlantic Ocean

Indian Ocean

Pacific Ocean

warm surface current

cold deep current

Water vapor

In the next stage of the water cycle, water from rivers and oceans evaporates into water vapor. Liquid water evaporates when it is heated by the sun. Water vapor rises from the surface of rivers and oceans to form clouds.

Rain

Clouds

Rivers and oceans

Water vapor

evaporation

water vapor

liquid water

Water from hot water springs is heated from under the ground.

Evaporation

Evaporation is the process of a liquid changing to a gas. A puddle of water evaporates when it is heated by the sun. Where does the water go? It does not just disappear. The water evaporates when it is heated by the sun to become invisible water vapor in the air.

This lake became dry when all the water evaporated.

Clouds

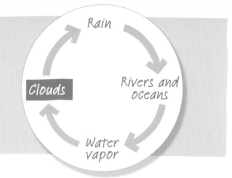
Water vapor changes into clouds in the next stage of the water cycle. Water vapor condenses into tiny droplets of liquid water as it rises and cools. The air temperature is lower the higher up you go. Many tiny droplets of water form clouds in the sky. The droplets are so small that the air can hold them up easily. As more water vapor condenses the clouds grow larger and heavier.

Large, dark heavy clouds soon drop their water as rain.

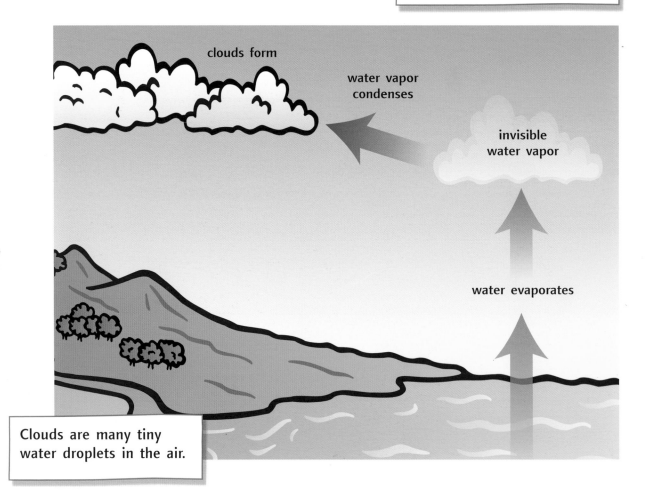

clouds form

water vapor condenses

invisible water vapor

water evaporates

Clouds are many tiny water droplets in the air.

16

Types of clouds

There are more than 100 different types of clouds swirling around in the wind over Earth's surface. Clouds are grouped according to their shape and their height above the ground. There are four main groups of clouds. They are cirrus, cumulus, stratus, and nimbus.

Miles above
Earth's surface

cirrus

cumulonimbus

6

4.8

Cirrus clouds are wispy, feathery clouds high above the ground.

3.6

Cumulus clouds look like balls of cotton wool and are middle level clouds.

cumulus

2.4

Nimbus clouds are low, black clouds heavy with water.

Stratus clouds are sheets of cloud low to the ground.

stratus

nimbostratus

1.2

Earth's surface

Any cloud with "nimbus" or "nimbo" in its name is a rain cloud.

Frozen water

What is freezing?

Freezing is the process of a liquid turning into a solid. Liquids freeze when they are cooled to a low enough temperature. Water expands as it freezes to form ice crystals. As it expands, ice becomes lighter than water and this is why ice floats.

Ice

Water freezes into ice when temperatures are at, or below, 32°F (0°C). Most of the fresh water on Earth is locked up in ice. Thick **icecaps** hold fresh water near the North Pole and South Pole. Fresh water is also locked up in **glaciers** and on mountain tops.

The poles of Earth are covered in thick sheets of solid ice, called icecaps.

Solid water, or ice, floats in liquid water.

18

Snow and hail

Water can fall from clouds in the sky as rain, or as solid snow, or hail. Snow and hail form high up in the sky at temperatures below freezing point. Here the water vapor freezes into solid ice instead of condensing into liquid water.

Snow is ice crystals that form around dust in the air. Partly melted snow crystals cling together to form light, feathery snowflakes.

Every snowflake has its own pattern of ice crystals.

Snow falls from the sky in light, feathery snowflakes.

The balance of nature

The balance of nature shows how the water cycle is linked with Earth's other cycles. Water has an effect on non-living and living things in every environment on Earth. The seasons, food, plants, rocks, and animals all help maintain the water cycle.

Food cycle

Seasons cycle

Plant life cycle

Water cycle

Animal life cycle

Rock cycle

The water cycle is an important part of the balance of nature.

Water and the seasons

The different seasons help move water through the water cycle. In many places, rising temperatures in spring cause snow and ice to melt. In tropical areas, large amounts of rain fall in the wet season. At the North Pole and South Pole, the seasons are cold, and water occurs mainly as ice.

As snow and ice melt in spring, many rivers begin to flow.

Water, rocks, and soil

Water flowing over Earth's surface changes the land. Moving water is one of the main causes of natural **erosion** of rocks and soil. Fast-flowing rivers carry rock **sediment** along, dropping it on flood plains as they slow down. Along coastlines, pounding waves wear away the cliffs and beaches.

Cliffs are slowly eroded by pounding waves.

Water and plants

Water is in every living thing on Earth, including plants. This makes water very important for the survival of plants.

Plants take in and lose water constantly. Some plants need more water than others to live and grow. A cactus in the desert can survive with very little water. Some plants, such as waterlilies, only grow where there is a lot of water.

Waterlilies grow on the edges of ponds and lakes.

Water and animals

Water is in the body of every animal on Earth. Many animals, such as whales and fish, spend their whole lives in water. Penguins, polar bears, and seals spend time in the water and on the sea ice. Some animals, such as frogs, live half their lives on land and half in water.

When they are not diving for fish, penguins are often seen on the sea ice.

Many animals and plants live and grow in rainforests where there is high rainfall.

Water and food

The amount of food in an area is closely linked to the amount of available water. Rainforest and deserts have very different amounts of food because they have different annual rainfalls.

Rainforests have high annual rainfalls, and provide food for a wide variety of plants and animals. In deserts, there is less food because there is very little rain.

Only a few plants and animals can survive in deserts with very little water.

People and water

People use water in different ways. Having a good supply of fresh water is important to daily life. However, people are polluting rivers and oceans, and using up fresh water supplies. This can affect the water cycle.

Polluting water

Water all over Earth is being polluted by human activities. Oceans, which hold the most water, are being used as garbage dumps. Oil spills pollute water and kill the animals and plants that live in it. Chemicals dumped into rivers pollute fresh water supplies. Garbage thrown onto the street goes down the drain and out to sea.

Oil spills cause a lot of damage to the environment.

Wasting fresh water

People are using up fresh water faster than it can be collected. In cities, fresh water mostly comes from rivers or **dams**. Pipes connect the water to taps in people's homes. Being able to turn on a tap makes it easy to waste fresh water.

Most city water comes from huge dams built on rivers to collect fresh water.

Water conservation

Water conservation is any process that helps clean and save fresh water. This includes using fresh water supplies carefully. Many parts of the world have limited water supplies. It is predicted that by 2025, two out of three people will not have access to fresh water. We need to conserve fresh water supplies to stop this from happening.

Many people have to travel long distances to collect fresh water.

Collecting rainwater

One way to increase fresh water supplies is for more people to collect rainwater. Rain is the main source of fresh water on Earth. Many people in country areas catch rainwater in large tanks. In cities and towns, tank water could help save tap water supplies. People everywhere can catch rainwater in tanks. As rain falls on any roof it can be collected using a system of pipes.

Water tanks in every home would increase water supplies.

Saving water

Everyone can help save water by using water wisely. Reusing and reducing how much water you use can help maintain fresh water supplies for the future.

Reduce water use

- ⟳ Take shorter showers
- ⟳ Turn taps off properly and fix leaky taps
- ⟳ Add **mulch** to garden beds to reduce water loss

Dripping taps can waste a lot of water.

Recycle and reuse

- ⟳ Reuse washing water and bath water on the garden
- ⟳ Collect waste water from the kitchen to water pot plants

Watering the garden with used bath water can help save water supplies.

Collect fresh water

Using your knowledge of the water cycle, you can collect water anywhere you need it.

What you need

- One empty jar
- A spade
- A plastic sheet
- Five rocks
- An area to dig—ask permission first!

What to do

1 Use your spade to dig a hole in the soil. Make the hole a bit deeper than the height of the jar.

2 Stand the jar in the middle of the hole. Pack some soil around its base so it will not fall over.

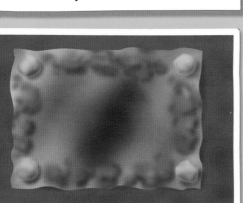

3 Cover the hole with the plastic sheet. Hold the sheet in place by putting a rock on each corner and soil along the edges.

4 Place a rock on the sheet directly above the jar. Leave it in place for a whole day. A hot, sunny day will work better than a cloudy day.

How much water is in the jar?

Where did it come from?

Living with nature

We all depend on the balance of nature for our survival. If people continue to disturb Earth's cycles, it will upset the balance of nature. Understanding Earth's cycles helps us care for Earth and live in harmony with nature.

"The Earth does not belong to us: we belong to the Earth."

(Chief Seattle Suquamish leader, about 1854)

Glossary

condenses	changes from a gas to a liquid
dams	strong walls built across rivers to hold water back
erosion	the wearing away of rocks and soil
evaporates	changes from a liquid to a gas
gas	matter that is light like air
glaciers	large masses of ice formed from snow over many years
gravity	the strong force that pulls things down toward Earth
icecaps	large masses of ice at the poles
liquid	matter that can flow like water
mulch	material, such as wood chips or compost, that stops water from evaporating from the garden
rain gauge	instrument that collects and measures the rainfall in one place
sediment	tiny pieces of rock
solid	matter that is hard and holds its shape
tropical areas	warm areas near the Equator (the imaginary line around Earth's middle)

Index